31143011295905
J B Zuckerberg, M
Weil, Jamie.
Mark Zuckerberg :

DISCARDED

Main

J

MARK ZUCKERBERG

Creator of Facebook

by Jamie Weil

Content Consultant
Anthony Rotolo, Professor,
S. I. Newhouse School of Public Communications,
Syracuse University

Core Library

An Imprint of Abdo Publishing
www.abdopublishing.com

www.abdopublishing.com

Published by Abdo Publishing, a division of ABDO, PO Box 398166, Minneapolis, Minnesota 55439. Copyright © 2015 by Abdo Consulting Group, Inc. International copyrights reserved in all countries. No part of this book may be reproduced in any form without written permission from the publisher. Core Library™ is a trademark and logo of Abdo Publishing.

Printed in the United States of America, North Mankato, Minnesota
092014
012015

THIS BOOK CONTAINS
RECYCLED MATERIALS

Cover Photo: Frederic Legrand/Shutterstock Images
Interior Photos: Frederic Legrand/Shutterstock Images, 1; Pablo Martinez Monsivais/AP Images, 4; Shutterstock Images, 7; Seth Poppel/Yearbook Library, 10, 15; Arne Hodalic/Corbis, 13; Elise Amendola/AP Images, 16; Rena Schild/Shutterstock Images, 19; Rick Friedman/Corbis, 22; Paul Sakuma/AP Images, 25, 45; Red Line Editorial, 26, 39; Eric Risberg/AP Images, 28; Marcio Jose Sanchez/AP Images, 31; Proehl Studios/Corbis, 33; Imagechina/AP Images, 34; Rich Schultz/AP Images, 37; Ben Margot/AP Images, 40

Editor: Arnold Ringstad
Series Designer: Becky Daum

Library of Congress Control Number: 2014944238

Cataloging-in-Publication Data
Weil, Jamie.
  Mark Zuckerberg: creator of Facebook / Jamie Weil.
    p. cm. -- (Newsmakers)
Includes bibliographical references and index.
ISBN 978-1-62403-647-7
1. Zuckerberg, Mark, 1984- --Juvenile literature. 2. Facebook (Firm)--Juvenile literature.
3. Facebook (Electronic resource)--Juvenile literature. 4. Webmasters--United States--Biography--Juvenile literature. 5. Businesspeople--United States--Biography--Juvenile literature. 6. Online social networks--Juvenile literature.
1. Title.
006.7092--dc23
[B]

2014944238

CONTENTS

MEETING THE PRESIDENT

Sweat was dripping down Mark Zuckerberg's face. It was April 20, 2011. In just minutes, the 26-year-old cofounder of Facebook would host President Barack Obama. They were holding an online version of a town hall meeting. In these events, people can ask politicians questions about important issues.

Obama's appearance at the Facebook town hall meeting demonstrated how important the social networking website had become.

The Facebook Campaign

Chris Hughes, Zuckerberg's college roommate and a cofounder of Facebook, worked for Obama. He used social media to get the word out about Obama's 2008 presidential campaign. This made it easier for Obama to communicate with young people, who often get news from the Internet rather than newspapers or TV.

Zuckerberg waited at Facebook headquarters in Menlo Park, California. He wore a jacket and tie. He only dressed this way for special occasions. Almost every other day of the year, he wore jeans and plain dark T-shirts. On cold days, he'd add a dark hoodie. Even as a billionaire, he preferred his own simple style instead of fancy clothing. Zuckerberg planned to give the president a Facebook hoodie as a gift.

When President Obama arrived, he shook Zuckerberg's hand. Obama opened the meeting by thanking Zuckerberg for hosting it on Facebook. Obama told the audience he was proud to be the guy that got Zuckerberg to wear a jacket and tie. Obama

For more than a decade, Facebook has changed the way millions of people communicate with their friends.

noticed how uncomfortable Zuckerberg was in his outfit. He suggested they should both take off their jackets and relax.

A New Way of Connecting

Obama selected Facebook for his town hall meeting because he recognized the website's importance. Zuckerberg changed the way the world communicates when he created Facebook. The website became

Facebook and Voting

One reason for politicians' interest in Facebook has been its proven impact on voting. During the 2010 elections in the United States, users could click an "I voted" button on their Facebook profile. Doing this told their friends they voted, although it wouldn't say which candidate they picked. Researchers found that an extra 340,000 people may have voted in 2010 due to seeing that their friends voted.

the world's most popular social networking service. Zuckerberg launched Facebook on February 4, 2004. By 2014 the site had more than 1 billion users. People exchanged photos, wrote about their lives, and shared videos. Facebook's stated mission is to make the world a more open place.

Obama realized the possibilities Facebook represented. The room he stood in could only hold a few hundred people, but he could reach millions of people through Facebook. He was the first president to use Zuckerberg's platform to address the world.

Early Life

Mark Elliott Zuckerberg was born in White Plains, New York, on May 14, 1984. He grew up in Dobbs Ferry, New York, not far from New York City. His parents, Karen and Edward Zuckerberg, were well-educated professionals. Karen, a psychiatrist, stayed home to raise Mark and his sisters, Randi, Donna, and Arielle. Edward ran a dental office in the family home. The office became the site of Mark's early adventures in computer programming.

EXPLORE ONLINE

Chapter One discussed the Facebook town hall meeting Mark Zuckerberg hosted in 2011. The article below includes more information about the event. Is the information given on the website different from the information in this chapter? How is it the same? How do the two sources present information differently?

Facebook Town Hall Meeting
www.mycorelibrary.com/mark-zuckerberg

CHAPTER TWO

A TALENTED STUDENT

n a 2011 interview, Mark's dad said Mark was a quiet young boy who liked math and science. When his dad introduced him to computer programming, Mark wanted to learn more. In 1996 he created a program called ZuckNet. The program let the family computers to talk to each other using instant messages. For example, Mark's dad could be notified easily when dental patients arrived.

Zuckerberg, *right*, was encouraged by his father, *left*, to begin programming computers.

To nurture his computer skills, Mark's parents hired a computer tutor named David Newman. Newman saw that the 11-year-old Mark was already a skilled programmer. He had a hard time keeping up with Mark. Soon after, Mark's parents enrolled him in the local college for advanced computer classes.

Making Games

Mark was passionate about building programs on the computer as early as elementary school. He liked to make his own video games. Artist friends would come over to his house. They would draw ideas for games, and Mark would program them.

School Years

Mark attended public high school for two years at nearby Ardsley High. There he developed a love for the classical languages of Greek and Latin. In his sophomore year, he applied and was accepted to a private boarding school called Phillips Exeter Academy in New Hampshire. He chose that school because of its good reputation in math and computer education.

Phillips Exeter is one of the best-known and most expensive schools in the United States.

At Exeter he enjoyed fencing, a sport in which players duel with swordlike weapons. His desire to build computer programs continued to develop. For his senior project, Mark and his friend Adam D'Angelo created a music program called Synapse. The program analyzed its users' music. Then it suggested new music they might like. Later programs

Fencing Champion

At Exeter, Mark became captain of the fencing team. In fencing, two players wearing protective gear attack and defend with swordlike weapons. Mark became quite good. In 2000 he attended a US Fencing Association conference. There he was named most valuable player. This was rare for someone as young as Mark.

and services such as iTunes, Pandora, and Spotify would use similar technology to recommend new music to users.

In 2002 Mark enrolled at Harvard University in Cambridge, Massachusetts. Mark studied psychology and computer science. He was interested in how people and technology connected. It was that interest, along with his passion for building computer programs, that led him to launch Facebook from his Harvard dorm room.

When Zuckerberg left Phillips Exeter for Harvard University, he was already an accomplished programmer.

CHAPTER THREE

CODE MONKEY

A t Harvard Zuckerberg sometimes wore a T-shirt with the words "code monkey" written on it. This shirt identified him as a computer coder. This is a person who builds computer programs. Zuckerberg was most interested in the intersection between how people behave and how computer programs affect that behavior. He worked on many programs for fun. One that took off

Zuckerberg lived at Kirkland House at Harvard, one of the living spaces for undergraduate students.

Zuckerberg's Personality

Zuckerberg has been described throughout his life in many different ways. He has been called quick thinking, quick acting, and quirky. His future wife, Priscilla Chan, remembered thinking of him as nerdy when they met at a Harvard fraternity party. One reporter noted his warm presence and quick smile. Reactions to Zuckerberg differ depending on who is talking about him.

was called Facemash. Facemash searched Harvard's computer networks for photos of students. Then it presented two photos to the user. The user picked the person they thought was more attractive. The website used these choices to rank students by attractiveness.

Harvard students reacted and used it right away. The Harvard administration also reacted. Zuckerberg got in trouble. He was put on probation because he had offended some people. He had also taken the student images without asking.

The Winklevoss twins later competed in rowing at the 2008 Summer Olympics in Beijing, China.

Thefacebook

After seeing Facemash, three Harvard students asked Zuckerberg to help create a social networking website. They called the site Harvard Connection. The students were Divya Narendra and twin brothers Cameron and Tyler Winklevoss. At first Zuckerberg agreed, but he later changed his mind. He moved ahead with a new project: Thefacebook.

It was once common for universities to have paper directories called face books. They included photos of students. Their purpose was to help students get to know each other. Zuckerberg thought about how this activity could be done online. He shared his idea with his roommates. They decided to sit down and make it happen.

On February 4, 2004, Zuckerberg launched thefacebook.com out of his dorm room in Kirkland House. The service was open only to Harvard students. People needed a Harvard e-mail address to join the website. Users could figure out who they shared classes with and connect with their network of friends. Thefacebook became a huge hit. In 2005 the social network dropped the word *the* from its name and became Facebook.

After the website launched, the students behind Harvard Connection said he stole their idea. Zuckerberg said his idea was different from theirs. Narendra and the Winklevoss twins sued Facebook. Facebook ended up giving them an estimated $65 million settlement to end the lawsuit in 2008.

Zuckerberg posted the message below on his Facebook page on February 4, 2014, Facebook's tenth anniversary. He reflects on why he and his friends were the ones to build Facebook:

> I remember getting pizza with my friends one night in college shortly after opening Facebook. I told them I was excited to help connect our school community, but one day someone needed to connect the whole world.
>
> I always thought this was important—giving people the power to share and stay connected, empowering people to build their own communities themselves.
>
> When I reflect on the last 10 years, one question I ask myself is: why were we the ones to build this? We were just students. We had way fewer resources than big companies. If they had focused on this problem, they could have done it.
>
> The only answer I can think of is: we just cared more.
>
> Source: Mark Zuckerberg. "Today is Facebook's 10th anniversary." Facebook. Facebook, February 3, 2014. Web. Accessed August 13, 2014.

Point of View

After reading this post, reread the description of Facebook's founding in Chapter Three. How does Zuckerberg's post shed new light on his actions in 2004? What message is he trying to get across to his audience in 2014?

CHAPTER FOUR

WELCOME TO SILICON VALLEY

By summer break of 2004, Facebook had grown significantly. Zuckerberg decided to leave Harvard and move to Silicon Valley. This is an area in California between the cities of San Francisco and San Jose. Many technology companies have offices there. Facebook's quick growth showed Zuckerberg he had found something people wanted.

After building Facebook at Harvard, Zuckerberg decided he had to move to California to grow the website.

He needed to see how big his company could grow. Facebook would take all his attention.

He moved to a town called Palo Alto. There, he and his friends at Facebook rented a house. They threw wild parties, but there was also serious work happening. Zuckerberg and his friends set up computers next to each other and would write code all night long. This is where "hackathons" were born. The idea was that a person could program something incredible in just one night with focus and creativity. Hackathons are a tradition still practiced at Facebook today.

Hacking

The word *hack* in *hackathon* refers to the idea of hacking. Hacking was originally known as the process of creatively using programming to solve problems. Today *hacking* often refers to people illegally accessing computer networks.

The Young CEO

Zuckerberg was only 19 when Facebook launched. He had never had a job. Many questioned whether

Zuckerberg refused to sell Facebook, preferring to build the company himself.

he could run a company that was growing so large so fast. Along the way, big companies sought to buy Facebook. Zuckerberg consistently rejected these offers. In 2006 he even turned down a $1 billion offer from Yahoo! Inc., a major Internet company.

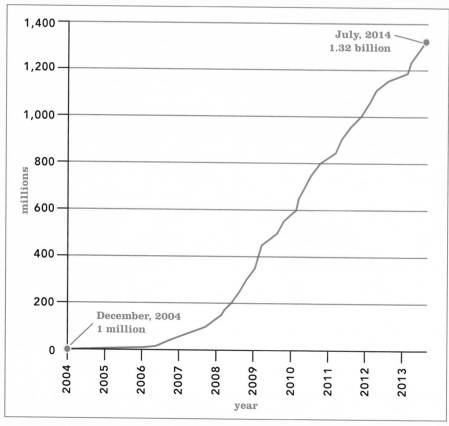

Number of Facebook Users

This graph shows how the number of Facebook users has grown over the years. Where on the graph did Yahoo! offer $1 billion for the company? Based on the graph, do you think Zuckerberg made the right move by turning down the offer? What would you have done, and why?

Facebook investors recommended Zuckerberg seriously consider the $1 billion offer for the company. They explained that because he owned a large portion of the company, he could earn a huge sum of money from the deal. According to one key investor, Zuckerberg responded that he was not in it for the money. He simply wanted to build the best social networking site.

FURTHER EVIDENCE

Much of this chapter involves Zuckerberg launching a business with his friends. His stated goal was to create a program that changed the ways friends connect. If you could pick out a main point from this chapter, what would it be? Check out the website below. Does the information support the main point in the chapter?

Launching Facebook
www.mycorelibrary.com/mark-zuckerberg

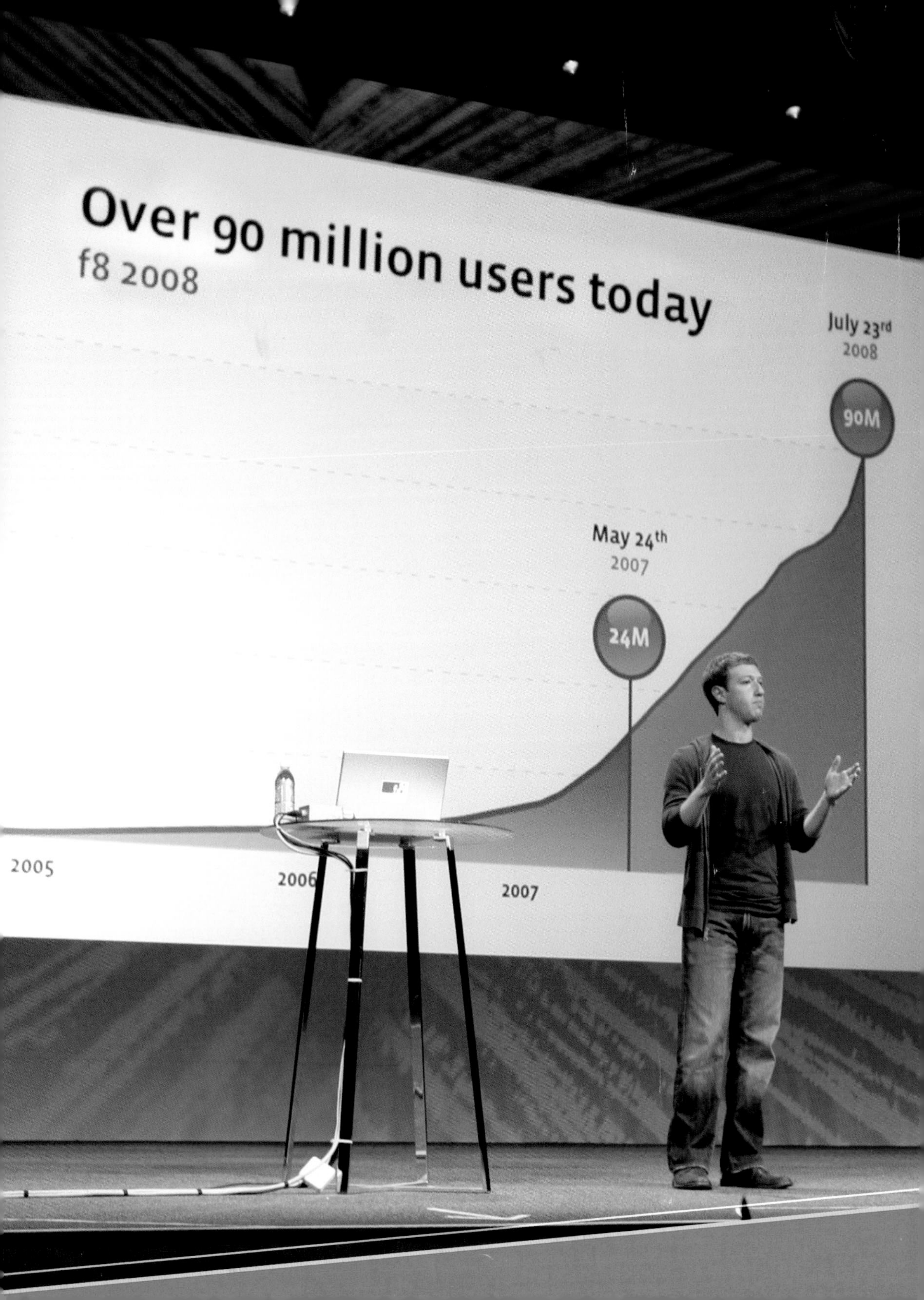
Over 90 million users today
f8 2008
July 23rd
2008
90M
May 24th
2007
24M
2005
2006
2007

CHAPTER FIVE

FACEBOOK'S PROFILE

By 2007, one year after Zuckerberg turned down the offer from Yahoo! Inc., Facebook had grown to 50 million members. It had not been the first social networking website, but it was quickly becoming the largest. The increased number of members meant Facebook needed more money to operate. When the huge technology company

Zuckerberg's decision to move to California paid off as the number of users and investors grew.

Microsoft offered to invest $240 million in Facebook, Zuckerberg took the deal.

This was a turning point for the company. Zuckerberg could now build the infrastructure he needed to keep up with Facebook's growth. Over the next few years, the company added more features to Facebook. People liked some features, but users often complained when the website changed in appearance. Even so, membership boomed.

Privacy

Facebook members value privacy. Member privacy became a major issue for Facebook as the company grew. Users wanted to make sure only approved people could view their posts and photos. Many preferred to avoid showing their information publicly. Users could adjust their privacy settings. Still, many complained these settings were too confusing.

Zuckerberg knew members were concerned with privacy. He also knew Facebook's future relied on advertising income. In 2007 he introduced Beacon, a

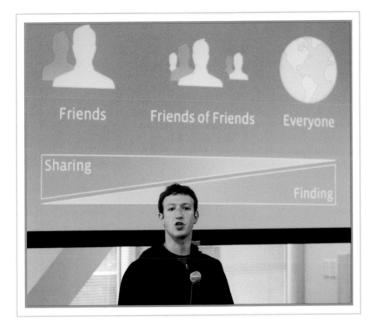

An outcry from users forced Facebook to take privacy concerns seriously.

program that would gather details about members' web-browsing habits. That way, advertisers would know how to target customers. It backfired. Some Facebook users were furious, especially when a few of them found their entire holiday gift list posted on their public Facebook profile. The program was cancelled in 2009.

Living and Working in Silicon Valley

By 2010 Facebook had 500 million members. Because Facebook grew so fast, the company continued

Person of the Year

In 2010, at age 26, Zuckerberg was named *Time* magazine's "Person of the Year." In just six years, he had connected more than half a billion people. He had created an entirely new system of communicating. Facebook changed the way in which people related to their friends.

to outgrow its offices. Though the buildings have changed, certain things have stayed the same. For example, there are few walls in the office space, so employees can see each other. Comfy couches and chairs are arranged next to the desks. The floors remain slick and uncarpeted. Workers can use bikes to move around quickly.

In 2011 Facebook moved to its new headquarters located at One Hacker Way in Menlo Park, California. The area was named a wildlife habitat, which means the many foxes that surround the headquarters can mill about freely. The employees love the foxes. Workers snap shots of them and post them on a Facebook page dedicated to the animals.

Facebook's vast headquarters in Menlo Park houses more than 2,000 employees.

Zuckerberg is known for his relatively simple lifestyle. He dresses in casual clothes and does not frequently show off his wealth in public. However, in May 2011, Zuckerberg bought a $7 million home near his office. In 2013 he heard a real estate developer was trying to buy a nearby house. Zuckerberg bought all the houses surrounding his. He then rented his neighbors' homes back to them. This gave him more control over his privacy.

CHAPTER SIX

SETTING GOALS

Facebook's success can be linked to Zuckerberg's goal-setting habits. Zuckerberg shows his willingness to step outside his comfort zone through unique personal and business goals. For several years, he has set one major goal each year. In 2009 he decided to wear a tie every day. In 2010 he decided to learn Mandarin Chinese for a trip to China. In 2011 he vowed to eat only meat from

Zuckerberg visited China with his longtime girlfriend, Priscilla Chan, in early 2012.

animals he killed personally. In 2012 he decided to spend more time writing computer code. In 2013 he set a goal to meet a new person outside Facebook every day. In 2014 he vowed to write a personal thank-you note every day.

In 2012 Zuckerberg married his longtime girlfriend, Priscilla Chan. They owned a dog named Beast and lived in the upscale neighborhood of Crescent Park in Palo Alto, California. Chan graduated from medical school a few days before their marriage.

Philanthropy

Zuckerberg has emerged as a major philanthropist. In 2010 he signed an agreement called the Giving Pledge. People who sign the Giving Pledge promise to give more than half of their money to charity. Zuckerberg often posts about his charitable contributions on his Facebook page.

Both Zuckerberg and Chan have shown their commitment to giving money to support education. On May 29, 2014, they announced a $120 million

Zuckerberg spoke alongside Newark mayor Cory Booker at a press conference about his donation in 2010.

donation to schools in the San Francisco Bay Area. Prior to that, Zuckerberg had donated $100 million to Newark Public Schools after meeting the mayor of Newark, New Jersey, at a fundraiser.

Making his Mark

Zuckerberg and Facebook have grown up together. The company's motto was originally "Move Fast and Break Things." This value was important to Zuckerberg when he started the business at 19 years old. The idea was to make new things and get them into the world as fast as possible, even if mistakes were made along the way. In 2014, the new motto became "Move Fast with Stable Infra." *Infra* is short for the word *infrastructure*. Zuckerberg wants to minimize mistakes and keep the company growing.

By July 2014, Facebook was worth approximately $192 billion. In a midyear report to investors, the company said that 1.32 billion people check their Facebook page at least once each month. Of those, 829 million people use the website every day. Those

Company	Value	Year	Description
WhatsApp	$19 billion	2014	Instant messaging service
Oculus VR	$2 billion	2014	Virtual reality headsets
Instagram	$1 billion	2012	Photo sharing service
Face.com	$100 million	2012	Face recognition software

Facebook Acquisitions

This chart shows some of Facebook's largest acquisitions, along with a brief description of what each company does. Does the value of any of these companies surprise you? How might these companies fit with Facebook's vision of connecting people?

users spent an average of 40 minutes each day on Facebook. The vast majority of people used mobile phones to access the service.

In its ten-year history, Facebook has purchased several other Internet and technology companies. These purchases have been designed to help the company's mission of connecting people. One of its biggest purchases was WhatsApp in 2014. This

In 2014 Zuckerberg emphasized the importance of mobile apps and devices in Facebook's future.

service lets users send instant messages using phones. Facebook paid $19 billion for the company.

More than a decade after starting Facebook, Zuckerberg wasn't slowing down. If the first ten years of the company have been any indication of what he is capable of, the next ten years may bring even more dramatic changes to the way people communicate online.

From the beginning, Zuckerberg has stated his vision is to connect the world. He says getting people on the Internet is critically important:

> When people have access to the Internet, they can not only connect with their friends, family and communities, but they can also gain access to the tools and information to help find jobs, start businesses, access healthcare, education and financial services, and have a greater say in their societies.
>
> A recent study . . . found that the Internet is already an important driver of economic growth in many developing countries. Expanding Internet access could create another 140 million new jobs, lift 160 million people out of poverty, and reduce child mortality by hundreds of thousands of lives.
>
> Source: Mark Zuckerberg. "Connecting the World from the Sky." Internet.org. Internet.org, March 28, 2014. Web. Accessed August 13, 2014.

Changing Minds

Imagine you make a friend from the Amazon rain forest who is opposed to having an Internet connection in her village. How might you change her mind? Write a proposal convincing your friend the Internet will improve her life.

IMPORTANT DATES

1984
Mark Elliott Zuckerberg is born on May 14.

1996
Zuckerberg creates ZuckNet to connect his family's computers.

2000
Zuckerberg attends Phillips Exeter Academy.

2007
Facebook membership reaches 50 million.

2010
Zuckerberg is chosen as *Time* magazine's "Person of the Year."

2011
Barack Obama becomes the first president to have an online town hall meeting on Facebook.

2002

Zuckerberg and classmate Adam D'Angelo develop Synapse Media Player.

2002

Zuckerberg enters Harvard University.

2004

Zuckerberg launches Thefacebook from Kirkland House at Harvard University.

2012

Zuckerberg marries his girlfriend, Priscilla Chan.

2013

Zuckerberg buys the neighborhood surrounding his house to ensure privacy.

2014

Zuckerberg turns 30, and Facebook turns 10.

STOP AND THINK

Take a Stand

This book discusses how social media websites such as Facebook have changed the way the world communicates. Do you think these new ways of communicating have made the world more open and connected? Write a short essay explaining your opinion. Make sure to give reasons for your opinion, including facts and details that support those reasons.

Dig Deeper

After reading this book, what questions do you still have about Mark Zuckerberg and how he's changed the world? Write down one or two questions that can guide you in your research. With an adult's help, find a few reliable sources about Zuckerberg that can help answer your questions. Write a few sentences about how you did your research and what you learned from it.

Say What?

Understanding the technology world can mean learning a lot of new vocabulary. Find five words in this book that you've never heard before. Use a dictionary to find out what they mean. Then write the meanings in your own words, and use each word in a sentence.

You Are There

Zuckerberg has pledged to give the bulk of his earnings to charity. Imagine you have billions of dollars. What do you do with that money? Do you spend it? Do you save it? Do you share it? How would your core values affect your decision?

GLOSSARY

classical
from the ancient Greek and
Roman periods

infrastructure
the computers and
networks that handle the
behind-the-scenes work of
major websites

intersection
where two things meet

philanthropist
a person who shares his or
her money through charitable
contributions to important
causes

probation
a period of time during which
a person is closely monitored
after being given a warning
for questionable behavior

psychiatrist
a medical doctor who
specializes in helping people
with mental illnesses

quirky
odd and different in ways
that stand out to others as
unusual

reputation
what people think or judge
about the overall quality of a
person or a thing

LEARN MORE

Books

Williams, Mary E. *Mark Zuckerberg*. Detroit, MI:
Lucent Books, 2013.

Woog, Adam. *Mark Zuckerberg: Facebook Creator*.
Detroit, MI: KidHaven Press, 2009.

Websites

To learn more about Newsmakers, visit
booklinks.abdopublishing.com. These links are
routinely monitored and updated to provide the most
current information available.

Visit **www.mycorelibrary.com** for free additional tools
for teachers and students.

INDEX

ABOUT THE AUTHOR

Jamie Weil is a writer who lives in a small rural town in Northern California. She's found many old friends and made new friends on Facebook. She especially appreciates it when her husband and her kids like her posts.